Colours

Written and devised by
David Bennett

Illustrated by
Andy Cooke

I like black, black is best.

Black is dark,
Like the night.
Black goes really
Well with white.

Who am I?

I like red, red is best.

Red is bright,
Rich and loud.
Red stands out
From the crowd.

Who am I?

I like yellow, yellow is best.

Yellow is light,
Like the sun.
Yellow makes me
The pretty one.

Who am I?

I like blue, blue is best.

Blue is cold,
Like the sea.
Blue is great,
Just like me.

Who am I?

I like orange, orange is best.

Orange is warm,
Like a flame.
Orange is strong...
And I'm the same.

Who am I?

I like green, green is best.

Green is fresh,
Like leaves in spring.
On this green leaf
I croak and sing.

Who am I?

I like brown, brown is best.

Brown is muddy,
Like a puddle.
My fur is brown
And soft to cuddle.

Who am I?

I like pink, pink is best.

Pink is gentle,
Soft and pale.
Chicks like to swing
On my pink tail.

Who am I?

I like grey, grey is best.

Grey is dull,
Like a cloudy day.
But grey is lively
When I'm at play.

Who am I?

I like all colours,
All colours are best.
I'm the colours
Of all the rest.

Who am I?